MW01487664

DIETRICH BONHOEFFER

A Life from Beginning to End

Copyright © 2019 by Hourly History.

All rights reserved.

Table of Contents

Introduction

A Happy Childhood

Bonhoeffer during World War I

The Making of a Great Theologian

A Student of Life

Doctor of Philosophy

Pastoral Career in Barcelona

Bonhoeffer Heads to America

Resistance against the Nazi Party Begins

Imprisonment and Execution

Conclusion

Introduction

In the face of ruthless totalitarian rule, it is only the rare few who stand up at risk of their own life to do what is right. Dietrich Bonhoeffer was one of those exceptional individuals. Even on pain of death, he would not bend, he would not budge—this German pastor fought the Nazi regime with every fiber of his being.

In the end, Dietrich Bonhoeffer would be one of countless victims executed in German concentration camps before the conclusion of World War II. But he would not go unnoticed. Bonhoeffer left a legacy of moral courage and resistance which continues to inspire people to this day. His book *The Cost of Discipleship* is considered a modern classic, and Bonhoeffer is one of only two people to have been recognized as a martyr by the United Methodist Church since the Reformation of the sixteenth century. Thanks to his undying determination to stand up for his beliefs, Dietrich Bonhoeffer will live forever and be remembered as a brave hero of a dark time in German history.

Chapter One

A Happy Childhood

"The blessedness of waiting is lost on those who cannot wait, and the fulfillment of promise is never theirs. They want quick answers to the deepest questions of life and miss the value of those times of anxious waiting, seeking with patient uncertainties until the answers come. They lose the moment when the answers are revealed in dazzling clarity."

—Dietrich Bonhoeffer

Dietrich Bonhoeffer came into this world on February 4, 1906, in the quiet, neatly kept German town of Breslau. Today Breslau lies in what is considered part of Poland, but in the early twentieth century it was quintessentially German. Dietrich was born during the heady days of the German Empire when a self-confident Germany was on the rise a few decades after the unification of Germany in 1871.

Dietrich's birth was followed mere minutes later by his twin sister Sabine. The proud parents of these newborn twins were Karl and Paula Bonhoeffer. Dr. Karl Bonhoeffer was a deeply respected psychiatrist who stood toe to toe with the likes of Sigmund Freud, on several occasions challenging and refuting the famed psychoanalyst's theories. Dietrich's mother Paula was also a well-respected member of the community. She hailed from an aristocratic family, but her easy demeanor rarely betrayed her blue blood roots.

Dietrich was born into a large family and had a total of seven siblings, but it would be to his twin sister Sabine that he would be closest. Growing up it was often with Sabine that Bonhoeffer confided his philosophical yearnings and thoughts. They even had a little game that they played together before they drifted off to sleep; as they lay nestled under the covers in the bedroom they shared, the twins would attempt to imagine what eternity might be like. Such thoughts may sound profound for a six-year old, but that was the way Dietrich Bonhoeffer was wired. It is said that his interest in these existential questions first began when he witnessed a funeral procession headed to a cemetery. This sparked in Bonhoeffer a curiosity about concepts such as life, death, and eternity. Most people spend their life trying not to think of death, but for Bonhoeffer death held a special fascination. What happens when we die? What is the afterlife really like? From an early age, Dietrich Bonhoeffer couldn't help but think about such things.

But around the time that he and his twin sister were six years old, he had some more pressing things to consider as the family prepared to make a big move from Breslau to the German capital of Berlin. Karl had just been given a new professorship at the University of Berlin. Dietrich would later recall that his sister Sabine was excited about the move as if it were a great adventure, but that he on the other hand had his doubts. Little Dietrich had always been a sheltered child, and he was often fearful and apprehensive of change.

It was in late 1912 that the Bonhoeffer family arrived in Berlin. It took Dietrich a little bit of time to adjust, but not long after their arrival, he began to become quite enamored with the city. Rather than fear the new urban setting, he became enthralled with all the sights the city had to offer. He especially became a fan of the Berlin Zoo, spending several hours there with his family, watching exotic animals such as tigers, lions, gorillas, and giraffes.

In Berlin, the Bonhoeffer dwelling was located in the district of Grünewald. It was a three-story house, a bit large by most standards but just right for the Bonhoeffer family which consisted of eight children. Shortly after settling into their new home, the family celebrated the birthdays of young Dietrich and his twin sister Sabine on February 4th. Now that Dietrich was seven years old, it was determined that it was time for him to attend school with other local children at the Friedrichs-Werder Gymnasium. Prior to his enrolment at Friedrichs-Werder, Dietrich had been dutifully home-schooled by his mother.

Dietrich found himself terrified of the idea of going to school, and the fact that his twin sister would not be there with him only made him more uneasy. Dietrich was supposed to walk to his new school by himself, but Paula, showing concern for her rather timid son, ordered one of the family's household employees to join him under the special provision that they were to walk on the other side of the street so as not to embarrass Dietrich in front of his schoolmates. Luckily, Dietrich's uneasiness as a new pupil at the school quickly evaporated as he fell into the groove of both studying and socializing with his fellow classmates. Soon he was excelling academically, and life at the school became second nature, or as his father remarked at the time, "Dietrich does his work naturally and tidily."

Nevertheless, Dietrich was always happy when school let out as the occasion would coincide with family holidays to the college and resort town of Tübingen. Dietrich was enthralled by the picturesque trappings of Tübingen whose gothic architecture seemed to evoke a magical time in European history. During their vacation time, the children were often regaled with fairy tales as they hiked through what could only seem to be enchanted forests, hills, and mountains of the scenic region. It was during these forays into the wilderness that Dietrich first learned how to hunt, a pastime that his family was eager to pass down. Dietrich appeared to be a good marksman but, according to one childhood account, after he killed a falcon with one single shot, Dietrich burst into tears and put his gun down. Dietrich, who often openly speculated about matters of life and death, was horrified at the thought that it was his own hand that had abruptly ended a life. He had come face to face with the possible end result of aggression, and he did not like what he saw.

Gunshots would similarly interrupt Dietrich's peace of mind during another family excursion when on July 28, 1914, their vacation was interrupted by word of the start of an all-out conflagration in Europe—the First World War had begun.

Chapter Two

Bonhoeffer during World War I

"We have been silent witnesses of evil deeds: we have been drenched by many storms; we have learnt the arts of equivocation and pretence; experience has made us suspicious of others and kept us from being truthful and open; intolerable conflicts have worn us down and even made us cynical."

—Dietrich Bonhoeffer

The spark which lit the global conflagration of World War I was ignited by a single man. On June 28, 1914, Gavrilo Princip, a young Serbian revolutionary, assassinated Archduke Franz Ferdinand of Austria while he was visiting the Bosnian city of Sarajevo. This event would eventually drag several world powers into a conflict in which each one would have to choose sides.

Germany, due to both official and unofficial agreements, would inevitably side with Austria-Hungary. Austria-Hungary and its allies would form the Central Powers, which consisted of Austria-Hungary, Germany, Bulgaria, and the Ottoman Empire. This block of belligerents would face off against the Allied Powers of France, the United Kingdom, Russia, Italy, Japan as well as the United States, Serbia, Belgium, Greece, Montenegro, and Romania.

As this powder keg began to explode, regular German households such as the Bonhoeffers were frequently engaged in lively discussions at the dinner table about the political intrigue and military happenings. Like many children his age, Dietrich was at the time enthralled by the idea of soldiers marching off to battle. During the early days of the war, he would often act out scenes of warfare with Sabine and their younger sister Susanne. However, Dietrich and his siblings were to get an early dose of the horror of warfare when Lothar, their cousin, came home from the Western Front. Sabine later recalled that Lothar came back from the war "half blinded and limping on crutches" with his "head and legs swathed in bandages." This certainly served as a visceral reminder of the true cost of such a conflict.

Striking the Bonhoeffers even closer to home was the enlistment of their eldest son, Karl-Friedrich, followed by the next oldest son Walter. Both were sent to serve in the German infantry. It must be noted that for a family as affluent as the Bonhoeffers, military service was most certainly a choice and not a necessity. Overcome with the patriotic fervor in Germany at the time, Dietrich's older brothers were indeed more than happy to enlist and serve their country. Such sentiment was to the great sorrow of their mother Paula, not because she disbelieved in the German cause for war, but out of the worry and heartache that all mothers feel when their children march off to battle. Sadly, her worst fears would be realized a few years later when she received a telegram which coldly announced the death of young Walter. He had apparently sustained an injury from an explosion, and even though he survived the initial blast, he perished from the resulting infection.

Although the entire family grieved the loss of Walter, for Dietrich the death had direct philosophical consequences. He found himself asking why a good and benevolent God would allow his brother to die. Dietrich would eventually reach his own conclusions, but for his parents the more immediate concern was over Dietrich's two remaining older brothers. The oldest son Karl-Friedrich was still stationed on the Western Front, and his fate was a source of severe stress for the entire household. This worry was then compounded even further when the only other son of fighting age left the family to aid the war effort. This left Dietrich alone with only his sisters for company. It would remain this way until the war finally came to an end in November of 1918, allowing Dietrich's older brothers Karl-Friedrich and Klaus to return to the grateful arms of their parents.

The war to end all wars was over, but its aftermath would prove to have long-lasting repercussions for the Bonhoeffer family, the German nation, and eventually the entire world.

Chapter Three

The Making of a Great Theologian

"The ultimate test of a moral society is the kind of world that it leaves to its children."

—Dietrich Bonhoeffer

After a complete defeat in World War I, Germany would be forced to pay a heavy price for its involvement in the war. The Treaty of Versailles that brought the war to a close exacted heavy reparations upon the German government which put a tremendous strain on the economy. As unemployment soared and the shelves of local stores became uncomfortably empty, young Dietrich, who was used to a life of comfort, immediately noticed the difference. Particularly distressing during these trying times was the fact that turnips had become standard fare at dinner. It may not seem like much, but turnips were normally used as horse feed back back then, and many Germans felt humiliated that they had become desperate enough to eat what they considered animal food.

The war had taken a toll on the Germans in just about every aspect of their lives. It was during these depressing times that young Bonhoeffer sought to find his true vocation in life. He had been a budding musician for several years, and his parents were convinced that he would some day become a concert pianist. But although Bonhoeffer was good at the keys, he wasn't a child prodigy by any means, and he also wasn't all that interested in becoming a professional musician. Dietrich's heart was elsewhere, and when an expert pianist arrived from a local conservatory to critique his abilities, he fell short of everyone's expectations. It was then that Bonhoeffer revealed to his family his true ambition in life: he wanted to become a pastor.

This great reveal provoked mixed responses from Dietrich's relatives. There was some precedent for it as family members had previously been involved with the church, but in more recent times the Bonhoeffers were much more dispositioned toward academia than they were toward the clergy. While Dietrich's mother was supportive, his father was indifferent at best, on one occasion remarking that it was a pity that Dietrich would choose to devote his time to such a quiet and uneventful field. But Dietrich's stubborn persistence eventually got his father to reconsider. At one point during a conversation with his son on the matter, even after deriding theology as a "dead field," Karl went on to inform his son, "I suppose that if anyone can resuscitate a dead field, it may be someone as determined and as spontaneous as you, Dietrich."

Dietrich would indeed persevere and continue to seek out his dream of being a theologian. Wishing to encourage her son, Paula started attending church with Dietrich and were there to support him during his confirmation. Upon seeing how serious he was, she gave him her blessing along with a token of her esteem—the Bible of his slain sibling

Walter. Walter had apparently kept the Bible with him at the Western Front, and it had been by his side when he died. Dietrich would forever treasure the Bible and take it with him everywhere he went from then on. Walter's Bible would serve to remind him of why he kept the faith.

Soon after Dietrich's realization of his preferred profession in life, the German post-World War I drama reached its climax when in early 1921 the Allied Powers successfully pressured Germany to agree to pay some 132 billion Reichsmarks in reparations. Dietrich Bonhoeffer was 15 years at the time of this economic catastrophe. But although cash-strapped and bankrupt Germany had been given a heavy load, as long as Bonhoeffer held fast to his inner dreams of teaching and preaching to the world with all of his might, any burden imposed on him by the wider world was managable.

Chapter Four

A Student of Life

"Cheap grace is the preaching of forgiveness without requiring repentance, baptism without church discipline, communion without confession, absolution without personal confession. Cheap grace is grace without discipleship, grace without the cross, grace without Jesus Christ."

—Dietrich Bonhoeffer

Bonhoeffer finished his basic schooling in March of 1923, and upon passing the mandatory exams required for admittance to college, he enrolled at the prestigious University of Tübingen at the age of 17 in order to pursue a degree in theology.

Soon after his arrival at Tübingen, Dietrich was initiated into a prestigious college fraternity called the Hedgehogs. According to Bonhoeffer's later recollection, he was rather reluctant to join the fraternity, but after being approached by members who were impressed with his pedigree, he was convinced that it would be in his best interest to take part. Bonhoeffer would come to regret this decision, however, when he discovered the anti-Semitic tendencies of the group. This fact was made clear to him one day when he was studying in the university library and was approached by a fellow student who noticed him wearing his fraternity jacket.

Eyeing his jacket, the student sat down next to Bonhoeffer and remarked, "I just wanted to comment on the nice jacket you are wearing." Dietrich is said to have then replied, "Why, thank you—it's a Hedgehog jacket." The other student nodded soberly, "I know." At which Dietrich inquired, "Oh, are you a member?" which provoked amusement in the youth before he flatly explained to Bonhoeffer that he was the head of the Jewish student group on campus. Dietrich, still not making the connection between being Jewish and being a Hedgehog, replied, "I'm afraid I don't understand." This then prompted the young man to bluntly inform Dietrich, "I'm sorry, but I believe that the Hedgehogs would rather have a dog join their fraternity than a Jew." This poignant exchange would stick with Bonhoeffer for the rest of his life, opening his eyes for the first time to the disparities and discrimination that existed within the world he lived.

Newly enlightened as he was, Bonhoeffer began to long for a more liberal and accepting institution. This was achieved after just one year at Tübingen when he opted to transfer to the University of Berlin. He found the big city campus of Berlin to be much more accepting and open-minded than the elitist atmosphere prevalent at Tübingen. At the University of Berlin, academic ability was prized over the prestige of fraternities and social clubs. This was something that Bonhoeffer welcomed whole-heartedly as he wished to immerse himself in his studies more than anything else. He also greatly admired and enjoyed his professors who were said to be some of the best in the world when it came to matters of theology.

Nevertheless, Bonhoeffer was never afraid to question these masters of the subject, and once he became a bit more engaged in the classroom, his instructors began to take note of just how adept Dietrich was in matters of theological philosophy. Bonhoeffer began to befriend and have quite frank discussions with his professors, hammering out the intricacies of such things as Johann Wolfgang von Goethe's critiques of modern civilization and the primal nature of man. His teachers were duly impressed by Bonhoeffer's ability to comprehend such complexities of thought, and Dietrich was soon pegged down as a young man who indeed had the wherewithal to become a great theologian.

During his college days, Dietrich Bonhoeffer had for the most part approached theology from a solely intellectual perspective. Even though he was fully dedicated to the mysteries of God and the universe, it was all a very much cerebral pursuit. However, his heartstrings would finally begin to be pulled during a summer outing with his brother Klaus in Rome, Italy.

Here, in what many consider the cradle of Catholicism, Bonhoeffer would have a major spiritual awakening. At first, he simply occupied his time with seeing the sights of the city and visiting all of the hotspots of culture and history that Rome had to offer. Soon he began to take note of the religious fervor of the city. He saw people lining up for mass at all hours of the day, and he began to realize that for many Italians, religion was more than abstract thought; it was a vital part of everyday life. Bonhoeffer came to the conclusion that the Catholic system used rituals and sacraments to bring the average person into daily contact with the divine. He felt that this expressive fervor was something that European Protestants had lost, leading them down the road of a much more dull, analytical approach to their faith.

During his foray into the Roman Catholic Church, Bonhoeffer was also impressed by the diversity he witnessed. During a visit to St. Peter's Basilica, he was amazed to see Italians, Russians, Greeks, French, and Brits all singing the same Latin hymnals. Thinking back on his experience in German Protestant churches, Bonhoeffer began to feel that they were small, provincial, and narrow-minded in comparison. As it turns out, this student of the church had his notebook with him that day, and he recorded his findings in four words, "universality of the church."

This was the beginning of a theme of unity that Dietrich would carry with him and speak passionately about for the rest of his life. But as much as he enjoyed this universal brotherhood that the Catholic Church seemed to exude, he still found plenty of faults. In one instance, he witnessed a little boy entering a confessional to confess his sins. Shortly after the boy left the confines of the priest's confessional, Bonhoeffer saw the same child suddenly turn in horror and run back as if he had suddenly remembered an unconfessed sin. It was in seeing a sight like this that Bonhoeffer began to see error in the practices of the Catholic Church. As he put it, Bonhoeffer believed that God forgives all sins, spoken and unspoken, of a repentant believer.

After Bonhoeffer had his fill of Italy, he and his brother Klaus hopped on a boat, sailed across the Mediterranean, and landed in Libya which was under Italian control at that time. If Bonhoeffer was impressed with Rome, he was even more wide-eyed and amazed as he walked through the North African city of Tripoli. He wrote home about his amazing adventure in the exotic marketplaces of Libya where for the first time he encountered Bedouins and Arabs. Although Bonhoeffer enjoyed his experience with these Libyan locals, he was deeply dismayed at the behavior of the occupying Italian soldiers whom he deemed to be oppressive and at times much too vulgar toward the local population.

Dietrich and his brother Klaus were very sympathetic to the local residents and, after befriending a few of them, gained access to parts of Libyan life to which most visitors were not privy. On one occasion, the Bonhoeffer brothers were allowed to attend a service at a local mosque, an apparently awe-inspiring experience of which Dietrich would later note, "It would really be very interesting to study Islam on its own soil to prove more fully the cultic and social aspects of the religion." The rest of Dietrich's time in Libya remains rather mysterious until its abrupt end in May of 1924.

At this point, Dietrich had apparently fallen ill and was suffering from some sort of gastrointestinal distress. He was obviously not at his best under such conditions, and while under this duress he and his brother had somehow run afoul of the Italian authorities in Libya. Although the exact cause is not specified, Dietrich references their sudden departure and being quickly taken "away in an officer's car as unwelcome guests." Despite the drama of his exit, Bonhoeffer was equal parts amazed and humbled by what he had seen and experienced in Libya, and he would treasure the excursion for the rest of his life.

Chapter Five

Doctor of Philosophy

*"The Christian, however, must bear the burden of a
brother. He must suffer and endure the brother. It is only
when he is a burden that another person is really a brother
and not merely an object to be manipulated. The burden of
men was so heavy for God Himself that He had to endure
the Cross. God verily bore the burden of men in the body of
Jesus Christ."*

—Dietrich Bonhoeffer

Upon his return to Germany, Bonhoeffer stopped to visit
with his parents. It was then that he learned that his 18-
year-old twin sister Sabine was engaged to be married to a
man named Gerhard Leibholz. A few years older than
Sabine, Gerhard was finishing his Ph.D. in legal philosophy
and appeared to have his act together. Nevertheless, due to
Karl Bonhoeffer's belief that no girl should marry before
the age of 20, the engagement would have to last at least a
couple of years before the pair could officially be married.

The Bonhoeffers liked Leibholz, but there was some
concern over his Jewish background. Although Gerhard
was a converted member of the Lutheran Church, he still
had   relatives—including   his   grandmother   and
grandfather—who went to synagogue and openly practiced
Judaism. Sabine's mother Paula was deeply concerned

about the social implications that this would have in a Germany where powerful strains of anti-Semitism existed just below the surface.

Despite these deeply enshrined social misgivings, Sabine's parents fell in love with Gerhard almost as much as Sabine had. They were impressed with both his kindly manner and his intellectual interests. As Karl Bonhoeffer would admit at the time, "Of all these young people who now come to the house, I really like talking to young Leibholz best of all. He is both intelligent and unpretentious." For his part, Dietrich received Leibholz as his future brother-in-law with great joy and with open arms. All the same, he would feel a twinge of sadness at the idea of his twin sister getting married. He knew that as Sabine took on the role of wife, the closeness that they had shared would have to give way. Dietrich could feel that tight bond that only twins can know begin to finally unravel.

Shortly after Sabine's twentieth birthday in February of 1926, Sabine and Gerhard became husband and wife at the Grünewald Evangelical Church. The reception held at the Bonhoeffer home afterward was extravagant, with expensive decorations, classical dance music, and men and women dressed in their very best. As food and wine flowed freely, the evening was destined to become a grand celebration. After the festivities were over and everyone went their separate ways, Dietrich would remain in his parents' home for the time being as he continued his studies at the University of Berlin.

Studying was Bonhoeffer's primary choice of activity in life during this period, a decision that would allow him to produce a 380-page treatise called *The Communion of*

Saints in 1927. This tremendous academic paper elaborated upon the theme of the universality of the church, which Bonhoeffer had first conceived during his trip to Italy. Here he argued that Christianity needed to be more than a mere institution but rather a wellspring of the human soul and condition. Instead of being a place to visit on Sunday mornings, Bonhoeffer stressed that the Christian church should be at the very center of an individual's life.

After successfully defending his treatise in public in December of 1927, Bonhoeffer graduated and received his doctor of philosophy degree at the tender age of 21. Now with a degree in hand, Dietrich Bonhoeffer was ready to put theory to practice.

Chapter Six

Pastoral Career in Barcelona

"Who can really be faithful in great things if he has not learned to be faithful in the things of daily life?"

—Dietrich Bonhoeffer

In 1928, Bonhoeffer was given an assistant pastorship over a church in Barcelona, Spain. He would be helping Fritz Olbricht, a 45-year-old German pastor who preached to a small group living in the Spanish city.

Initially, Bonhoeffer's family was against the idea of him setting out to do pastoral work and instead encouraged him to continue his academic education. Dietrich was eager to get out into the world, however, and being an assistant pastor in a place like Barcelona was a good way for him to start an independent life. Even so, Bonhoeffer dithered and only left home after two weeks of farewell parties with family and friends. Once he did leave, he did not travel directly to Spain but instead made a stopover in Paris, France to spend a few days sightseeing in the French capital.

Upon his arrival in Spain on February 14, 1928, Dietrich was amazed at the diverse and eclectic mix of classes and peoples that he encountered. He could not help but feel that the diversity of Spain was much different than the rigid hierarchy that he had left behind in Germany. Here, he thought, he could finally implement his universal church. But despite Bonhoeffer's best efforts, neither the church members nor the pastor whom he was assisting seemed too interested in his ideas of how things should be run. Bonhoeffer's complex theoretical preaching sometimes rubbed others the wrong way, and when he took the platform to speak, most had a hard time comprehending what he said.

Nevertheless, Bonhoeffer persevered and was soon was given a regular appointment as a Sunday School teacher. At first, attendance was exceedingly low, but after Bonhoeffer went around the local neighborhoods knocking on doors and spreading the word about his class, he was able to elicit enough interest to get a decent group of students to attend. Many came merely to witness the spectacle of the young German with his excited speech and his funny-looking Panama hat preaching to them.

Still, Bonhoeffer fell in love with the working classes during his time as assistant pastor in Barcelona and found that his true calling was to help poor parishioners such as these. When one of his regular church members, a woman he referred to as Frau Richter, shared with him her burden of a troubled adult son who lived with her, he saw it as his duty to help. Frau Richter's son was a regular rounder at the bar scene in Barcelona, and the woman wished for Dietrich to speak with him and convince him to repent for his drunken ways. Bonhoeffer dutifully agreed to meet with the young man and, showing up at the residence, he coordinated with Frau Richter to counsel her son. After drinking coffee and eating pastries with Bonhoeffer, Frau Richter went to the back of her house to rouse her son, who was sleeping off his latest round of drunkenness.

Dietrich heard a man's voice arguing with the woman before she came back to report, "I'm sorry, Josef is incorrigible today. You would never know that he is a twenty-three-year-old man. He acts like a spoiled child of six." At the mother's request, Bonhoeffer then went to the young man's room to address him but, as he was about to enter, Josef got up of his own accord and walked right by Dietrich and into his mother's kitchen asking, "Is there any coffee, mama?" apparently ignoring Dietrich's presence outright. Dietrich was insistent, however, and following the man to the kitchen, he poured him a cup of coffee and began to engage him in conversation. He asked the young man to go to his church on Sunday, but Josef replied that he was busy. Dietrich had a clever counter-argument to this, telling the man that it was unsafe for his mother to walk alone to church. Bonhoeffer then reminded Josef that since he was the man of the house (his father had already passed), it was up to him to make sure his mother got home safely.

It was through inventive angles such as these that Bonhoeffer found a way to get to the hearts and minds of his parishioners. Rather than preaching some stale message about why the man should put down the bottle and join the church, Dietrich found a way to reach his subject's conscience and get him to come around. He learned to meet people—both metaphorically and literally—exactly where they were.

Chapter Seven

Bonhoeffer Heads to America

"If you board the wrong train, it is no use running along the corridor in the other direction."

—Dietrich Bonhoeffer

After his stint in Barcelona, Bonhoeffer made his return to Berlin in 1929 in order to take a few post-graduate courses. It took him a little time to get acclimated to the rigors of academia again after having spent time in the more relaxed atmosphere of Spain. Soon enough, Bonhoeffer was back in the swing of things. He even became reacquainted with his old philosophical sparring partner, a man named Franz Hildebrandt, whom he had first met at the University of Tübingen. Often diametrically opposed in viewpoint, the two would have lively debates in class and soon became close friends.

Among one of the most important debates that Bonhoeffer would kick off in his post-graduate studies was the question of how to prove God exists. This, of course, has been a concept that just about all thinkers, theologians, and philosophers have been seeking to come to grips with from the dawn of time. Encapsulating this debate was Bonhoeffer's latest academic powerhouse of a paper entitled *Act and Being*, in which he argued that the church had become too cerebral in its approach, and it was this cold intellectualism that was stifling faith in a real and present God. His work was once again generally well received, and he was acknowledged as a gifted theologian.

On the heels of this acclaim, Bonhoeffer was contacted by the Union Theological Seminary in New York. The school greatly appreciated Bonhoeffer's efforts and desired for him to come to New York City to study at their seminary. Always excited to experience the spiritual proclivities of new lands, Bonhoeffer jumped at the chance. Not wasting any time, he boarded a ship called the *Columbus* in 1930 and headed for America.

As soon as his ship came into port on American shores, Bonhoeffer was shocked by the massive magnitude of the New York skyline, which even in 1930 was a sight to see. Always the eager tourist, Bonhoeffer made sure that he paid his respects to Times Square, Carnegie Hall, and Broadway. But as excited as he was to see such fantastic New York mainstays, once he settled in at the university, he found his lodging to be rather lacking. Much more cramped together than he was used to, the residents of the dorm tended to keep their doors wide open so that students could easily converse with each other. This open-aired style was in direct contrast to Bonhoeffer's private, almost monkish habits of study.

Bonhoeffer would adjust, however, and soon he would form his own group of friends at the school. Of these, a young student named Frank Fisher who hailed from Harlem would prove to be one of Bonhoeffer's most important friends as he introduced him to African American culture and spiritual life. On one occasion that Bonhoeffer would always treasure, Fisher took him to visit the Abyssinian Baptist Church, an African American church situated in the enclave of Harlem, New York. Immediately after Bonhoeffer stepped inside the door, he was amazed at the passion and enthusiasm that the building contained. He heard people chanting, singing, and moving about the church with full emotive expression. He fell in love with the worship style that he encountered and would later recall that his time in the Abyssinian Baptist Church was the one moment that he "experienced true religion in the United States." Bonhoeffer was so enamored by the church that he began teaching Sunday School there. Just as was the case during his stint in Spain, he was soon a favorite faculty member of the church among the parishioners.

Yet, along with the great spiritual awakening he experienced, Bonhoeffer also encountered the uglier side of the discrimination that was rampant in America at the time. This was experienced in the most visceral sense when his friend Fisher invited him to celebrate Thanksgiving with relatives of his who lived in the American South where racial segregation was in full force. Bonhoeffer would later write to his family about the experience, expressing his amazement at just how racially compartmentalized everything was. As he put it, "The conditions are really rather unbelievable."

Here Bonhoeffer witnessed every aspect of life quantified and categorized by race. Your skin color determined what train you got on, what dry cleaner you went to, what restaurant you dined at, and even what public water fountain you drank from. The bizarre intricacies of segregation in the Deep South horrified Dietrich and made him relieved to return to New York. However, shortly after his return to New York, Bonhoeffer read some rather distressing newspaper reports of happenings back in his own country. He was informed of a new political group gaining in prominence in Germany called the National Socialist German Workers' Party, whose unmitigated brutality would come to shock the world like no other.

Chapter Eight

Resistance against the Nazi Party Begins

"We are not to simply bandage the wounds of victims beneath the wheels of injustice, we are to drive a spoke into the wheel itself."

—Dietrich Bonhoeffer

When Bonhoeffer returned to Berlin in the fall of 1931, he found that the atmosphere had changed considerably. On campus of the University of Berlin, he attempted to start a new group in which to debate philosophical concepts but soon found a level of oppression against free speech that he had not encountered before. Bonhoeffer also discovered that anti-Semitism on campus was more prevalent than he ever remembered it being, with some students even being attacked physically. Nazi party leader Adolf Hitler had indeed grown to prominence, and Bonhoeffer was distressed to find students beginning to use what would later become the infamous greeting of Nazi Germany, "Heil, Hitler!" If Bonhoeffer caught a student using the expression, he would quickly remind them that God was the only entity worth such esteem.

Meanwhile, Dietrich continued giving lectures at the university and soon became one of the regulars on the lecture circuit, frequently speaking to over 200 pupils at a time. Yet as much as he enjoyed his lectures at the university, Bonhoeffer once again sought to find an audience more in need of his ministry. He found it in the form of a confirmation class for boys located in a particularly rough side of Berlin. Bonhoeffer received quite a welcome on his first day of teaching this course—he was preparing for class dressed in his Sunday best when suddenly bits of trash began to fall down on top of him from above. He looked up to find some of his prospective pupils above him emptying cans of rubbish. Seeing his surprised reaction, these youngsters burst into boisterous laughter. Bonhoeffer quickly regained his composure and simply turned and entered the room where the Sunday School was scheduled to be held. His harassers went right in with him, close on his heels, intent on making fun of him even inside the classroom walls. Refusing to be provoked, Bonhoeffer surprised them with his passivity.

Once inside, he turned and addressed the crowd, speaking only in a soft voice that forced his tormentors to quiet down so that they were able to hear what he was saying. He informed the group that it was quite a show that they put on, but that he wasn't deterred. Next, Bonhoeffer began sharing his recent experience in Harlem, New York, where he had met young people just as destitute as they were, who struggled to succeed all the same. Before they knew it, the rambunctious students found themselves drawn in by Bonhoeffer's direct approach, and they were riveted by his oratory. Instead of causing trouble, they were now eager to sit down and listen to Bonhoeffer speak.

Always wishing to get to know his subjects as best he could, Dietrich moved into the poor district where his students lived, renting the second-floor room of a bakery. Some of his disadvantaged students took advantage of Bonhoeffer's new location above the bakery and frequently visited to have a meal with the pastor. Bonhoeffer was not one to turn anyone away; he was always generous with his charges, as was evidenced when the confirmation date for the students arrived. As it turned out, nobody had a decent set of clothes to wear. To provide his students with some nice dress clothes for the confirmation ceremony, Bonhoeffer purchased a huge bolt of wool and then handed it off to a suit maker to have a set of clothes ready for every single student who needed it.

Bonhoeffer was proud of his students, and on the day of their confirmation, he sought to give them strength by telling them that it was their faith that would provide them with the tenacity to proceed. As long as they held fast to it, there was nothing anyone could do to stop them. Sadly, as the Nazi Party grew in size and strength in the early 1930s, Dietrich Bonhoeffer and his students would frequently have to remind themselves of this great courage.

Dietrich's fortitude was on full display when Adolf Hitler was declared chancellor of Germany in 1933. Shortly after Hitler became chancellor, Bonhoeffer could be heard on the radio giving an address, in which he denounced the idea of a leader who called himself a *führer*. Bonhoeffer did not get the chance to finish all of his remarks, however, as the radio signal was abruptly shut off. It remains unclear whether this was a technical error or if the Nazi high command pulled the plug. Considering the circumstances, most believe it was the latter.

Soon after Bonhoeffer's radio address, on February 27, 1933, there was a fire in the German center of government, the Reichstag. A local communist leader was eventually apprehended and charged with the crime. Although the alleged arsonist would claim that he was the sole perpetrator of the incident, the Nazis insisted that the act was an offshoot of a much larger conspiracy centered around the complete undermining of Nazi leadership. In his role as chancellor, Hitler convinced President Hindenburg to suspend the constitution and declare martial law. This act voided the otherwise inalienable rights of German citizens against such things as unlawful search and seizure and curtailed freedom of speech even further.

Bonhoeffer was increasingly alarmed by these happenings and was determined to speak out against them, even if it meant making himself a target of the forces of the Nazi regime. At a hastily organized gathering of German pastors, Dietrich Bonhoeffer took a bold stand, extolling his fellow ministers to stand up to the injustices being carried out by the Nazis. He called upon them to "assist the victims" of government wrongdoing "even if they do not belong to the Christian community." Most took this statement to be referring to the Jewish citizens of Germany who were the most severely oppressed by the draconian measures undertaken by the Nazi regime.

In front of a stunned audience, Bonhoeffer risked his career—indeed his life—to air his views that the church had a duty to stand up to Hitler and his government. Sadly, his words only seemed to make his fellow pastors apprehensive at best. Shortly after Bonhoeffer had challenged his brethren in this manner, he was reprimanded by overseeing clergy, who flatly informed him that he must cease making political statements or be accused of treason.

Nevertheless, Bonhoeffer continued to encourage resistance throughout 1933. His overt rebellion soon earned him a visit from Germany's dreaded secret police, the Gestapo, on July 24, 1933. Their ultimatum to Dietrich Bonhoeffer was blunt and direct. He was told in no uncertain terms that he must stop making trouble or he would be sent to a concentration camp. The first concentration camp had opened earlier that year and was mostly occupied by political prisoners and petty criminals. No-one had yet conceived of the horrors that German concentration camps would one day become. Still, even before the Holocaust began, being forced to stay in a concentration camp would be a nightmare all the same.

In 1933, Dietrich Bonhoeffer managed to avoid this fate—not by ceasing and desisting as the German secret police had ordered but by skipping town. A position had opened up at a German church in Britain's capital of London, and Dietrich was selected as the right person to fill it.

Chapter Nine

Imprisonment and Execution

"We must allow ourselves to be interrupted by God."

—Dietrich Bonhoeffer

Entirely disillusioned with the willful ignorance of church leaders in Nazi Germany, Bonhoeffer decided to leave his home country and head for more receptive audiences in London, England. Just prior to his departure he had met with Gerhard Ludwig Müller, the official director of the Reichskirche—a national coalition of German churches that had pledged their allegiance to Hitler and his government. During the heated exchange that ensued, Müller interrogated Bonhoeffer about his beliefs. As Müller probed his motivations, Dietrich Bonhoeffer raised his voice in his own defense, but Muller refused to listen and quickly ended their conversation.

After hitting this brick wall of belligerence, Dietrich used his move to London as a means of continued defiance against Nazi oppression. In London, Bonhoeffer lived in a cramped apartment and pastored an equally small church composed of England's working class. But simply working as a lay pastor for the working poor was not all that Bonhoeffer was doing while in England. In time, he managed to become acquainted with those in the higher circles of London's society. Most importantly he befriended Bishop George Bell, a representative of the British Parliament's House of Lords, meeting with him for the first time in late 1933.

It was to Bell that Bonhoeffer confided what was going on in Nazi Germany. Alarmed by what he was told, Bell used his influence to inform the British public. He contacted *The Times* newspaper and, in his missive, laid clear the egregious abuses that the Nazi regime had inflicted upon both Christian and Jewish citizens of Germany. It wasn't long before George Bell's missive made front page news and was heard around the world.

Hitler and his supporters soon heard of this breach in their oppressive wall of silence, and they were none too pleased. The Nazis viewed anyone supplying such sensitive information to other countries as nothing short of a traitor, who would be promptly tried and convicted of treason. As there were a limited number of Germans in England at the time, it didn't take them long to figure out the source of this breach in their embargo on the truth.

After Bonhoeffer became the number one suspect in the leak, he was ordered to report back to Germany. Here he was made once again to pay a visit to the Reichskirche. He was presented with a piece of paper and told it was a pledge of compliance. Signing would indicate that he agreed not to communicate with any other church or in any way speak negatively of Nazi Germany. Dietrich Bonhoeffer's act of defiance was simple yet dramatic: he shoved the paper away, stood up, and marched right out of the Reichskirche office. Instead of complying with the demands, Bonhoeffer blatantly refused to submit and continued to speak out against the German government at every possible opportunity.

It could not have been a more dangerous time to do so, as that summer had born witness to the "Night of the Long Knives." It was on June 30, 1934 that Hitler sent out Nazi storm troopers to systematically dispense with his political opponents. After the Night of the Long Knives, hundreds of German citizens lay dead, many for speaking out against the regime just as Bonhoeffer had done.

Bonhoeffer was spared for the moment, however, and in August of 1934, he attended a conference on the world alliance of churches held on the Danish island of Fanø. Here pastors from several countries met to discuss the state of the church. Of particular interest was the growing oppression in Germany. Bonhoeffer spoke passionately about the situation, stating to those assembled that they must act to aid the German church. He spoke of the need of shaking off complacency and rising to action, declaring that "there is no way to peace along the way of safety. For peace must be dared. It is itself the great venture and can never be safe." Bonhoeffer was deeply dismayed, however, when he found that most of those assembled figured he was embellishing the dangers posed to the church in Germany and simply did not take his claims seriously.

Close on the heels of this conference, on April 15, 1935, Bonhoeffer was given a new posting in an area in the remote northeast of Germany known as Pomerania. Here he gathered his remaining loyal adherents and sought to create a new theological bastion of resistance to the Nazi regime. Bonhoeffer and his fellow seminarians lived an existence very much akin to monks of the Middle Ages, spending their days in the countryside reading, writing, and perhaps engaging in some general physical exercise as they sought to prepare their minds and their bodies to take a stand against Hitler and his regime.

Always a prolific writer, Bonhoeffer used his time in Pomerania to write a book that would become his seminal masterpiece, *The Cost of Discipleship*. In it, Bonhoeffer laid out his plan of resistance as he extolled the faithful not just to believe but to take actions based on that belief. If this meant facing down a murderous regime of tyrants, Bonhoeffer pledged his willingness to do so.

Shortly after writing *The Cost of Discipleship*, Bonhoeffer was officially terminated as a faculty member at the University of Berlin. In fact, he was not only terminated but outright banned and told that he would not be allowed to teach or even speak freely in public at any future engagement in Berlin. Bonhoeffer would continue writing and speaking through whatever channels he could muster, however, never backing down in the face of oppression. His continued defiance would lead to his arrest by the German secret police, the Gestapo, on January 11, 1938. After a lengthy questioning session, he was released, but he was only let go on the condition that he must never set foot in Berlin again.

It was a month later in February of 1938 that Dietrich was first informed by his brother-in-law Hans von Dohnányi of a plot by the military intelligence outfit called Abwehr to overthrow Hitler. Bonhoeffer, who was at heart a pacifist, now found himself having to rationalize violence as he collaborated with a group intent upon Hitler's demise.

In the midst of this philosophical and moral wrangling, Bonhoeffer again left Germany in the summer of 1939, this time to return to the shores of America. Here he reconnected with the Union Theological Seminary in New York. It was generally the hope of his friends on both sides of the Atlantic that Dietrich would remain in the safe haven of the United States.

But much like Jonah, who according to the Bible got swallowed by a whale as a consequence of fleeing from his fate, Dietrich felt that he was only running from his destiny: "I have come to the conclusion that I made a mistake in coming to America. I must live through this difficult period in our national history with the people of Germany." He yearned to get back to the hot zone that Germany had become in the hope to save others from the coming destruction. Despite the danger, he bought a ticket to Germany, arriving back home in late 1939.

Here Bonhoeffer changed course and decided that, in order to be at his most effective in undermining the regime, he would have to be a kind of double agent. This meant he had to become a good actor and play his part well. He even began to—on occasion—express support for the Nazis to escape their suspicion. This sort of duplicity was on full display on June 19, 1940 when news came of the Nazi victory over France. Bonhoeffer was with a friend of his named Eberhard at an outdoor café when the announcement of this successful military campaign was made. Several Germans loudly cheered at the news and, to the astonishment of Eberhard, Dietrich was one of them. Bonhoeffer is said to have actually jumped to his feet and let out a passionate, "Heil, Hitler!" This, of course, was subterfuge on his part to keep the Gestapo off of his trail.

Meanwhile, Bonhoeffer worked tirelessly with his contacts to secure safe passage for quite a few individuals whose lives had been made forfeit by the Nazi regime. He also served as an important intelligence link between contacts in Great Britain, Norway, Sweden, Denmark, and Switzerland, keeping key players updated on the situation in Germany. Among these contacts, Dietrich would once again meet up with his old friend George Bell in May of 1942.

It would be the last time such a meeting was made before Dietrich Bonhoeffer was taken into permanent custody by the Nazis on April 5, 1943. Bonhoeffer had been linked to conspiratorial groups and the illicit transfer of money abroad, leading to his arrest by the Gestapo and his subsequent internment at Tegel military prison. At first, the conditions were bleak, with a shackled Bonhoeffer in a room with nothing more than a wooden bed and stool. But once word came through of his prominent connections, especially the fact that he had an uncle that was a jail warden, his treatment improved. Soon Bonhoeffer was unshackled and given books and writing materials. This allowed him to pen some of his greatest works even while behind bars.

Bonhoeffer was routinely interrogated during his stay at Tegel, but initially his interrogators failed to uncover the truth of his involvement with the Abwehr conspirators. This would all change, however, after a nearly successful assassination attempt on Hitler's life on July 20, 1944. Lieutenant Colonel Claus Schenk Graf von Staufenberg had placed a briefcase bomb underneath a table where Hitler was scheduled to meet with his associates. Staufenberg left the room before the bomb went off and made his escape. Although several others were killed in the ensuing blast, as fate would have it, Hitler survived the explosion.

From his prison cell, Bonhoeffer listened to Hitler's radio address shortly thereafter in which the Führer almost gleefully recounted his miraculous survival. Rather than taking out the Nazi dictator, the efforts would just lead to another round of Gestapo investigations, and soon enough, their inquiry would lead them back to Dietrich Bonhoeffer.

The beginning of the end for Bonhoeffer came when on September 20, 1944 Nazi detectives working on a tip discovered a stash of documents left at a military base by the conspirators. Inside these documents were found a few letters written by Bonhoeffer's own hand. These items clearly indicated Bonhoeffer as a member of the Abwehr conspiratorial circle.

In light of these developments, Bonhoeffer, who had previously been considered of little importance, was now considered a major threat. As such, on October 8, 1944, he was transferred to a high-security Gestapo penitentiary in Berlin. Just a few months later, in early 1945, Bonhoeffer was transferred from his Gestapo jail cell to the Buchenwald concentration camp. Even in the midst of the carnage at this death camp, Bonhoeffer urged the tortured souls around him to keep faith. Ever the itinerant preacher, Bonhoeffer moved from one group of inmates in the yard to another, seeking to encourage and sustain their flagging spirits.

In early April, Bonhoeffer was abruptly seized by the guards and forced to march out of the camp and into the back of a waiting van already overloaded with inmates. A decision had been made to transfer him to Flossenbürg concentration camp. Here, on the morning of April 9, 1945, Dietrich Bonhoeffer was stripped of his clothes and led naked onto the yard with some of his fellow inmates. He was made to step up onto a scaffold where a piece of rope was ready to be put around his neck. Bonhoeffer knew this was the end, but rather than show fear, if anything, he showed relief. For him, death would only be the beginning of the long and peaceful eternity that he had always dreamed about.

Conclusion

Just a couple weeks after Dietrich Bonhoeffer's execution, the entire camp would be captured by the Allies. One week after that, on April 30, 1945, Adolf Hitler would commit suicide. All of Germany would then surrender by early May. The fact that Nazi high command would expend so much energy and resources to execute prisoners such as Dietrich Bonhoeffer when utter defeat was just days away shows how depraved they were. Over the years, many have been saddened by the knowledge that if Bonhoeffer had been allowed to hold out for just a couple weeks longer, he would have been among those freed by the Allied liberation of the Flossenbürg camp.

But Dietrich no doubt wouldn't want anyone to feel that he had been cheated. For Dietrich Bonhoeffer, his life's mission had been fulfilled: he lived his life for God and gave the ultimate sacrifice in the end. Today, Dietrich Bonhoeffer is recognized by the United Methodist Church as a Christian martyr, one of only two people to have been bestowed this honor since the Reformation of the sixteenth century. His legacy as a man who practiced what he preached lives on and has inspired movements all over the world, ranging from the Civil Rights Movement in the United States to the anti-Apartheid movement in South Africa.

Made in the USA
Las Vegas, NV
15 February 2025

18177382R00024